IN HER OWN WORDS:

Time and circumstances permitting, I hopefully dreamt that if given all the opportunities I might fulfill my work to develop Lotusland to its maximum capacity into the most outstanding center of horticultural significance and of educational use.

— Excerpted from Madame Ganna Walska's will from 1984

REVISED EDITION 2020

We preserve and enhance the unique, historic estate of Madame Ganna Walska, care for and improve its collections, and develop its conservation and horticulture programs, so they educate us, inspire us, and advance our understanding and appreciation of the importance of plants in our lives and in the life of the planet.

Mission Statement

Ganna Walska
LOTUSLAND®

The Garden and its Creators

by Sharon Crawford

Acknowledgements
Photographs: Jessie Tarbox Beals, 22, (hand tinted by Peggy Lindt);
J.R. Eyerman, 28, 29 top, 30 right, 32 right, 33, 34, 35; Palmer Jackson Collection 19, 20 right, 26 top, 27;
Arden Stevens Collection, 23, 24 top right; Hania P. Tallmadge Collection, 6, 7, 8 right, 9 left,
11 top right, 12 left, 13 top, 15 bottom, 17 left, 18 top, 25, 46 left; Doris U. Jaeger, 9 bottom;
Eldon L. Tatsch, 32 top left; Santa Barbara Botanic Garden Archives, 24 left center;
Bob Craig; cover, inside cover, 1, 2, 3, 4, 5, 11, 26, 30, 31, 36, 37, 38, 39, 40, 41, 42, 43,
44, 45, 46, 47, 48, 49, 50, 51, 53, 54, 55, 56, back cover.
All other historic photographs and materials are from the Ganna Walska Lotusland Archives.

The author wishes to thank all the Lotusland staff, former employees and trustees who provided
valuable information. Special thanks go to Madame Walska's niece, Hania Tallmadge, who
graciously shared her aunt's attitudes as well as her extensive photographic collection.

ISBN 978-0-944197-47-9
Printed and Bound in Ventura, California by Jano Printing
Revised Edition, 2006
Second Printing, 2010
Third Printing, 2014
Fourth Printing, 2020

Contents

OPPOSITE: *Asian lotus graces the Water
Garden in summer.* TOP: *An Aechmea
inflorescence in the Bromeliad Garden.*
CENTER: Echinopsis 'Stars and Stripes'
in the Cactus Garden. BOTTOM: *Male*
Encephalartos *cone in the Cycad Garden.*

COLES PHILLIPS

Chapter One

Madame Ganna Walska – The Early Years

T HE EXTRAORDINARY WOMAN who was to become Ganna Walska had quite ordinary origins, born June 26, 1887 to Napoleon and Karolina Puacz of Brest-Litovsk, Poland. She was named Hanna, but her family called her Andzia. Her mother died when she was just nine; at adolescence her father sent her to St. Petersburg, Russia to live with an uncle, Canon Kazimierz Puacz, a professor at the Imperial Academy. In St. Petersburg young Hanna would become acculturated in the ways of a lady.

Perhaps she was too eager to learn; Hanna was still in her teens when she eloped with a Russian baron on June 13, 1907. Shortly after the wedding, her husband, Arcadie d'Eingorn, was diagnosed with tuberculosis. He claimed he would rather die than be shut away in a sanitorium for three years without her, so, to save his life, Hanna accompanied him to a sanitorium near St. Moritz, Switzerland. She dutifully obeyed the sanitorium's strict regime, but he did not. When she learned that he was sneaking out at night to drink and smoke with friends at the local tavern, she left him. The marriage was finally dissolved by the Russian Orthodox Church in 1915.

Returning to her uncle's home in St. Petersburg, Hanna met the man who was to inspire her opera career. In her autobiography, *Always Room at the Top*, she mysteriously refers to him only as "the second richest man in Russia." When she learned that the gentleman was honorary attaché to the chairman of the Imperial Opera House, she began attending the opera nightly, hoping in vain that he would notice her. Finally, she decided that the only way to attract his attention would be from the stage, as a singer. This was a much more momentous decision than it would seem today, for she had been raised with the belief that "nice girls" didn't go on stage. Rejecting her strict Catholic upbringing, she began to take singing lessons, first with Tartakoff of the Imperial Opera, and after 1914, in Paris with Jean de Reszke.

The name "Ganna Walska" occurred to her when she was scheduled to sing at a charity event. Separated from Baron Arcadie at the time, she couldn't use her married name on the program, yet it was considered improper for married women to use their given name publicly. The Russian version of "Hanna" was the more

1887–1915
CHILDHOOD
ARCADIE D'EINGORN
CAREER INITIATION

ABOVE: *Young Hanna at age nine with her father, dressed in mourning black after her mother's death.* LEFT: *Ganna Walska at thirty.* OPPOSITE: *Coles Philips painted the "Blue Portrait" in 1916; he selected Ganna as "the most individual among nine beautiful women of various nationalities.*

ABOVE: *Portrait of Ganna Walska's first husband, Baron Arcadie d'Eingorn. Right: The "Czar's portrait." According to Ganna Walska's memoirs, it was painted after the Czar of Russia selected her as the most beautiful woman present at one of his royal balls. After the Russian Revolution, Ganna Walska was able to purchase the portrait.*

exotic sounding "Ganna," and her rich imagination transformed her love for the waltz into "Walska." The title "Madame" was customarily used by opera singers, actresses, and married women.

In Paris, Ganna enjoyed some success as a cabaret singer while she continued to train her voice for opera. During this period she again encountered the man who unwittingly had instigated her singing career. Living frugally in Paris, having lost his fortune in the Russian Revolution, he was more interested in her at this time, but she found him much less attractive. When the first World War threatened Europe, Ganna took the advice of friends to visit America, assuming that the war would be over in a matter of months.

LEFT: *Ganna Walska in New York, 1916.* ABOVE: *Gana Walska and Dr. Fraenkel at the time of their marriage, and portrait of Dr. Joseph Fraenkel by Doris U. Jaeger.*

1915–1920
NEW YORK CITY
DR. FRAENKEL
LAUNCHING THE
CAREER

Ganna Walska was sufficiently fluent in French to obtain a position as a singer at the Century, a French theater in New York. A persistent throat problem sent her to Dr. Joseph Fraenkel, a renowned neurologist recommended by the theater's proprietor as "the only man able to help any difficult, hopeless or helpless case." She was puzzled and intrigued by the doctor's odd demeanor during her appointment. Only after they were married (a mere ten days later, on September 7, 1916) did Ganna learn Dr. Fraenkel had been smitten by her because of her resemblance to Alma Mahler, whom he had hoped to marry after Gustav Mahler's death.

Twice her age, Dr. Fraenkel called Ganna "Baby" and indulged her every desire to explore the world of music. Her days were filled with morning music lessons, luncheon musicales, opera matinees, and evening concerts. On February 18, 1918, she made her concert debut at a Biltmore Morning Musicale, sharing the bill with tenor Enrico Caruso and cellist Lucile Orrell. By December 1918 Ganna Walska was ready to launch her opera career with a performance in Havana, Cuba. This time she shared the

billing with the famous ballerina, Anna Pavlova. During her absence Dr. Fraenkel wrote frequent letters filled with assurances that she deserved success. The performance was, by her own admission, a disaster, but one poor showing could not deter Ganna. When she learned that Harold McCormick was in New York, she arranged a meeting with him, knowing that a generous portion of McCormick's International Harvester fortune went to support the Chicago Opera Company. Ganna rightly perceived McCormick as the key to performing with the Chicago Opera Company. She could not have dreamed in what manner her aspirations would be fulfilled.

Music didn't occupy every moment of Ganna Walska's life. During this period she began a long "search into the realm of mysticism," seeking from outside sources "the explanation of my existence." She attended seances, consulted the Ouija board, explored yoga, astrology, meditation, telepathy, numerology, Christian Science, and Rosicrucianism. For a brief period, she was convinced that she was the reincarnation of Catalani, a celebrated singer of Napoleon's era. In truth, the search for the meaning of

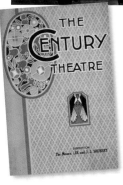

Mme GANNA WALSKA

CARNEGIE HALL
Seventh Ave. and 57th St., New York

SONG RECITAL
IN COSTUMES OF THE
SECOND EMPIRE
BY
GANNA
WALSKA
SOPRANO

Friday Evening
APRIL 6, 1934
at 8:45 o'clock

... PROGRAM ...

1. a. Caro mio ben..............................Giordani
   b. Der Kuss...................................Beethoven
   c. Warnung...................................⎫
   d. Un moto di gioja..........................⎭ Mozart
2. a. Pastorale................................Scarlatti
   b. Etude, C minor...........................Chopin
         Mr. Ross
3. a. Mondnacht..............................⎫
   b. Auf dem Wasser zu singen................Schumann
   c. Wiegenlied..............................⎫
   d. Die Post................................⎭ Schubert

— Intermission —

4. a. Das Mädchen spricht.....................⎫
   b. Blinde Kuh..............................⎪
   c. Von ewiger Liebe........................⎬ Brahms
   d. Willst du, dass ich geh.................⎭
5. a. Theme and Variations...................Corelli-Tartini-Ross
   b. Malaguena...............................Lecuona
         Mr. Ross
6. a. Ich hab in Penna einen Liebsten........⎫
   b. Elfenlied...............................⎬ Hugo Wolf
   c. Er ist's................................⎭

STUART ROSS at the Piano
Steinway Piano

Management, ANNIE FRIEDBERG, Fisk Bldg., 250 West 57th Street, New York

SCALE OF PRICES (incl. tax)   Lower Box Seats $3.30   Upper Box Seats $2.75
Entire Orchestra $2.75   Dress Circle $2.20   Front Balcony $1.65   Rear Balcony $1.10

THE 1920S

A DECADE OF
SUCCESSES AND
FAILURES

ALEXANDER COCHRAN

HAROLD MCCORMICK

ABOVE: *Alexander Smith Cochran in his yacht captain's uniform (top) and dressed for polo (center); a program from the Century Theater in New York, where Ganna Walska worked in 1915.* ABOVE RIGHT: *A 1924 issue of* Revue Internationale *featured Ganna Walska in an article highlighting contemporary women in the arts; a program for a song recital at Carnegie Hall in April, 1934 lists works by Mozart, Schumann, Schubert, Brahms, and Hugo Wolf.*

life was not really foremost in Ganna's quest, as she admitted:

> *... my pursuit was musical. The vital question for me was why I had strange difficulties with my singing.*

The comfortable existence as the pampered wife of a prominent physician left Ganna feeling somewhat restless. As she expressed it:

> *Though without the slightest degree of vanity, even then I did not feel quite in my right place, vaguely sensing that I could not always be known as the wife of a celebrity.*

Still, she was unprepared for the sudden end of that existence when Dr. Fraenkel died of a "stomach ailment" in April 1920, after a long period of suffering from excruciating night-time stomach pains. She cared for him at home until his final week, and after his death she was exhausted and devastated.

THREE MONTHS AFTER Dr. Fraenkel's death, when Ganna remained unable to sing because of her "black despair," close friends persuaded her to accompany them to Paris. They hoped that the change of scene would revitalize her desire to prepare for a performance with the Chicago Opera

Company, scheduled for the following winter. On board the *Aquitania* she recognized Alexander Cochran as a man she had noticed at New York social events; no doubt she also had read newspaper accounts calling him "the richest bachelor in the world," as sole heir of the Smith Carpet Manufacturing firm in Yonkers, New York. Although they encountered each other on board the ship, they never spoke until they were introduced on the last day of the voyage. They spent the afternoon together; after dinner he proposed marriage. She refused, and the next day he disembarked in London while she went on to Paris. He came to Paris a day later to propose again, and again was turned down. The same journey and entreaty occurred twice more that summer, and when she finally accepted, they were married that very afternoon, September 15, 1920.

Her regrets began almost immediately, when she realized that the real Alexander Cochran was not at all the man of her fantasies:

> *From the very first day of my marriage to Alec Cochran, I was so crushed by cruel reality that I was unable to even put up a fight to defend the image my illusion had created.*

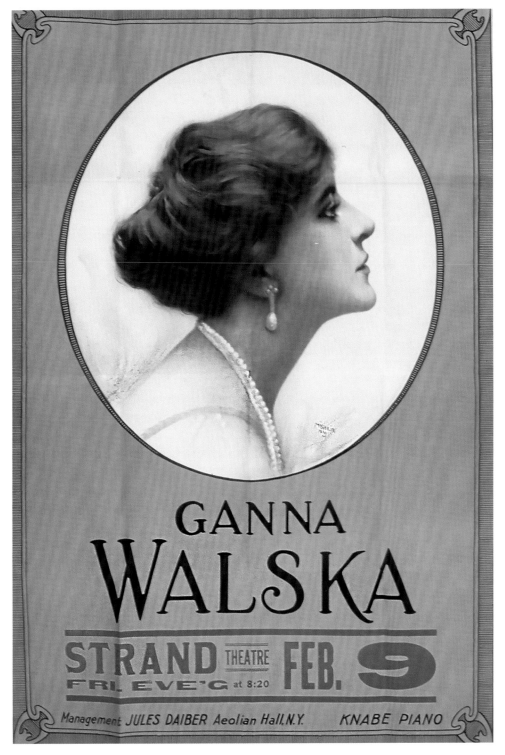

GANNA
WALSKA
STRAND THEATRE FEB. 9
FRI. EVE'G at 8:20
Management JULES DAIBER Aeolian Hall, N.Y.   KNABE PIANO

LEFT: *A large publicity poster for a New York Concert. Ganna Walska's publicist, Jules Daiber, used the original photograph by Mishkin and this drawing by Edward Simmons extensively during the 1920s.* ABOVE: *Ganna Walska with Harold McCormick in the mid-1920s (top) and a portrait of McCormick, President of International Harvester Company of Chicago.*

The real Cochran, "the most miserable man I have ever met," preferred playing hounds polo and riding in England, to spending time with his wife or furnishing their new home in Paris. He lavished her with gifts, but managed to present them in a manner she found insulting. Even worse, his jealousy over her career and her continued friendship with Harold McCormick forced her to cancel at the last minute her long-anticipated performance with the Chicago Opera Company in December 1920. Since she offered no explanation for her sudden departure from Chicago, the newspapers were filled with speculation. The inevitable and ugly divorce on May 29, 1922 gave more grist for the journalistic mills.

It was not by coincidence that Harold McCormick also had been a passenger aboard the *Aquitania* in June 1920. He was on his way to Switzerland to ask Edith Rockefeller McCormick for a divorce so that

ABOVE: *Ganna Walska in eighteenth-century French costume. She frequently purchased antique costumes and had them retailored in order to achieve her desired appearance for a role.* RIGHT: *Ganna Walska's costume for* Madama Butterfly, *designed and drawn by French couturier Erté, who designed many of her elaborate ensembles. This costume is now in the collection of the Los Angeles County Museum of Art.*

he would be free to marry Ganna Walska. The dissolution of marriage between the offspring of John D. Rockefeller and Cyrus McCormick, founder of International Harvester, was likely to cause headlines, but Harold was willing to take that risk; he had fallen in love with Ganna while she was still married to Dr. Fraenkel. Ironically, he received her telegram telling of her marriage to Cochran just as he was about to send her a cable announcing his freedom. McCormick flew to Paris immediately, showing up at their hotel the morning after the wedding. While Cochran slept in the next room, his bride served McCormick coffee and listened as he stated in a businesslike way, "Now you must divorce Mr. Cochran and we will be married as soon as possible."

McCormick patiently waited out Ganna's marriage to Cochran, careful not to have any

direct contact with her in order to forestall scandal. They communicated through her divorce lawyer, who was on McCormick's payroll. They tried in vain to avoid publicity when they were married in Paris in August 1922, but as she later wrote, "The stories of my divorce from Alec Cochran had hardly quieted down when those about my marriage to Harold McCormick began." Under the circumstances, the press couldn't resist a juicy story, and made the most of rumors and innuendo.

Ganna had to stay in Paris for the remainder of 1922 because of concert commitments in December and early January. Her French debut as a soloist in Beethoven's Ninth Symphony went so well that she decided to plan a concert tour in America. She hired a New York agent, Jules Daiber, who arranged for performances in thirteen US cities early in 1923. Unfortunately, Harold required an emergency appendectomy in early January, and the first half of the tour was canceled. She arrived in time to make her Carnegie Hall debut on January 29, sharing the bill with baritone Max Kaplick. Performances in Elmira, Detroit, Niagara Falls, Nashville, Greenville, and Boston were well received, but newspaper reviews were mixed. The headline in the Boston Globe generously declared:

WALSKA IN FIRST BOSTON
CONCERT REVEALS A VOICE OF
MUCH NATURAL BEAUTY. SINGER
WINS GREAT APPLAUSE.

But the writer went on to say that Madame Walska "manages to conceal most of her vocal resources from the casual listener" by her "attempts at singing in the coloratura style," for which he felt her voice was not suited.

During the concert tour Ganna and Harold made time for a second wedding in Chicago on February 13 (Harold's divorce had been in Illinois, which had a mandatory waiting period of six months between a divorce and remarriage). After a visit with Harold's mother in San Diego, Ganna returned to Paris for singing commitments and to attend to the daily operation of the Théâtre des Champs Élysées that McCormick had purchased for her.

Madame Walska's singing career had a few triumphs, but she was plagued by bad luck and subterfuge. Her Parisian opera debut in Rigoletto was spoiled by hissing in the audience; she blamed it on "some Russians" whose attempt to blackmail her had been thwarted. She bravely sang while ill in Berlin, and news of her poor performance received world-wide press coverage. A planned season with the Chicago Summer Opera at Ravinia Park was mysteriously canceled; she learned later that the manager had been bribed by Edith Rockefeller McCormick. Another problem arose. The now-famous Ganna Walska could never be sure whether an impresario wanted her name as a certain box-office draw–or because she could be relied on to bail the company out of any financial difficulties that might arise. She increasingly doubted that she was in demand for her singing talent, and continued to be troubled by periodic bouts of paralyzing stage fright.

From Ganna Walska's point of view, the publicity concerning her wealth was a disadvantage: "Being rich, people would never believe that I was earnest in my endeavors." On the other hand, she recognized that having money had enabled her "to create a center of music in Paris at the beautiful Théâtre des Champs Élysées." Conductor Walther Straram's symphony orchestra was considered the finest in Paris. She had the highest regard for Straram's musicianship and intellect. She felt she owed to him as her vocal teacher "everything I am today artistically, musically and literally speaking." For ten years she spent most of her time in Paris because only Straram could give her the confidence she needed to persist in singing, and Straram refused to go to America. Her devotion to him was so great that when he developed a fatal illness in 1931, she did everything in her power to prolong his life as long as possible. She not only financed a trip to a Swiss hospital for a series of experimental operations, she also traveled to Switzerland to provide him moral support during each of the painful surgeries and invited him to recuperate at her chateau in Galluis. When Straram died in November 1933, his son Enrich was able to take over the management of the theater, but could not bolster Ganna Walska's confidence as his father had.

During nine years of marriage to Harold McCormick, Ganna Walska made only three journeys to America, each occasioned by a concert tour. In 1925, Ganna declared, "I have returned to prove to the world that I have a real voice…" Having gone to great lengths to prepare for the role, she felt confident about the planned tour of "*Madama Butterfly*" with the San Carlo Opera Company. Her European tour of that opera had been very successful. In the *Musical Courier* for October 22, 1925, a full-page advertisement displayed a drawing of her Butterfly costume (designed by couturier Erté) surrounded by favorable reviews of her performances in France, Vienna, and Czechoslovakia. Then, inexplicably, Walska walked out of rehearsals in Chicago. The press made up stories about a rivalry with the mezzo-soprano, Stella de Mette, and a fight with tenor Franco Tafuro over a love scene in which she would not allow him to touch her costume. In their wildest speculations the journalists never guessed that Edith McCormick had quietly purchased the rights to all of the Puccini operas, and thus was able to block any opportunity Walska might

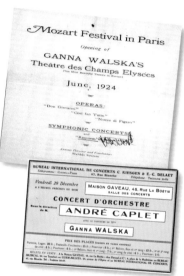

TOP: *Ganna Walska in a beaded gown, c. 1919.* ABOVE: *Handbills for Paris Concerts at the Théâtre des Champs Élysées and Maison Gaveau.*

13

TOP: *Ganna Walska with Walther Straram, at Galluis recovering from surgery.* ABOVE: *The Théâtre des Champs Élysées, a landmark building in Paris owned by Madame Walska for almost fifty years. She turned over the last of her shares to the theater in 1970 to assure a permanent home for the Orchestre de Paris.* RIGHT: *Château de Galluis with part of its formal garden.*

have to sing *Madama Butterfly* or any other Puccini opera.

The third American concert tour, beginning in December 1928, was more successful, although it began inauspiciously when an attack of influenza caused Ganna to cancel the first Chicago performance. After the rescheduled performance in Orchestra Hall, January 19, *The World* headlined: "Walska in Recital Ends Chicago Jinx. Forgets Operatic Setback, Gets Fine Reception." *The Herald Examiner* exclaimed "Ganna Sings; Scoffers Stay to Praise Her!" In the same paper, critic Glenn Gunn's review declared: "Dr. Gunn Lets Out A Secret: Ganna Can Sing!" As the finale of that concert, Ganna demonstrated her sense of humor and brought down the house with her encore rendition of "If No One Ever Marries Me." Despite rumors that McCormick had filled the hall by supplying free tickets to enthusiastic supporters, Ganna felt triumphant.

Ganna Walska made other headlines on this trip. Upon her arrival in New York, Ganna's traveling wardrobe and jewelry had been assessed by the US Customs authorities at $2,500,000, and an import duty of 80% on the jewelry and 60-70% on wearing apparel was demanded. Even after the items that had been purchased in America were allowed in, she threatened to take the case to the Supreme Court, insisting:

I am taking the customs fight to the Federal courts in order, as a feminist, to establish the principle that a woman's residence is where she lives and not where her husband lives.

The timing was perfect for Ganna to join in the National Women's Party fight for legislation that would allow American women the right to have residence independent from their husbands. The publicity surrounding her testimony before a Congressional committee undoubtedly helped the cause, and the legislation was passed. Harold McCormick supported her, but it must have been embarrassing to declare before a Customs authority that he and Ganna had made an oral pre-nuptial agreement allowing her to reside in France. After all the headlines, he may have been relieved when she returned to France in March 1929. McCormick was conspicuously absent when in October of 1929 Ganna Walska "opened the social season" with an extravagant party at the Château de Galluis that she had recently purchased. He did demonstrate his continued devotion by sending one of each type of International Harvester agricultural equipment, having them arrayed below her bedroom window before dawn on her next birthday.

Eventually, McCormick resigned himself to the likelihood that his wife would never come to live with him in Chicago. He filed for divorce on the grounds of desertion; it was granted October 10, 1931. Even after he remarried, he and Ganna remained on friendly terms. Years later she wrote,

> I lost him, if that phrase can be used to explain separation and divorce, but not in the real meaning of the word. ... Now, being above personal feminine vanity and selfish desires for my own happiness, I can touch his beautiful self and overlook completely those differences that separated us in an earthly way. I can love him now in a much nobler sense.

S INGLE AGAIN, and left without her mentor, Walther Straram, Madame Walska became introspective:

> Around forty I understood with a touching sadness that my dreams, those constant reveries conceived in the abstract, had not materialized. I realized that youth was already behind me ....

She gradually reached the conclusion that what she had previously considered "Bad Luck" was actually "directed from above and for a purpose–perhaps even for a Great Purpose." Aware of having achieved mental freedom and a great sense of independence, she wrote:

> I went back to the state I was in during a previous decade and soon found myself in a more or less profound search of the Truth.

A neighbor in Galluis introduced her to the works of Alexander Erskin and Dr. Cannon, both British advocates of hypnotism. Seeking answers, she went to England, but in her session with Dr. Cannon could not relax her suspicions enough to be hypnotized.

Madame Walska was very interested in the ideas of Paul Brunton, whose book *A Search in Secret India,* "definitively put my mind in the searching attitude." She was further inspired by his second book, *The Secret Path,* but when she met the author, she was disillusioned because he seemed such an ordinary man. Having read *Unveiled Mysteries* by Godfrey R. King, she journeyed to America specially to hear the author's inspirational lectures in Washington, D.C. Then, on the recommendation of a friend, she traveled to Chicago to meet a Master referred to only as "Mr. L." In this mysterious man she felt she had found at last "the personification of 'Goodness' in its highest form." Her euphoria was briefly deflated when he canceled a planned trip to New York to give her further instructions and bid her *bon voyage* before she sailed for Europe. But she forgave this human failure and thereafter accepted his wisdom through correspondence.

Between 1933 and 1936 Madame Walska spent approximately half of each year in France and half in America, using her New York house as the base for her travels to seek the elusive "Great Purpose" of her life. In the summer of 1936 she wrote, "Now there are no doubts within me!" Looking back on her life to that point, she concluded that her singing career had been inevitable:

> I see clearly that even if it had not been for that petty romantic, otherwise insignificant episode of my youth, the desire to express myself through the medium of singing would most certainly have come, perhaps in a different way.

Later that year, during a lesson with a new teacher, Ganna had a vocal awakening:

> I realized that the focal point of my thoughts, my so greatly desired goal was almost visible to me and now within my reach.

Studying with Madame Gilly,

> I knew I was right, ...I was assured the work of my life was singing and that it was my mission to express myself through my voice...

At this exalted point in her life, Ganna Walska felt that at last she had reached a level of "serene stability." She saw that her worst enemy had been her "excessive emotion,"

TOP: *Indian mystic Meher Baba (with moustache) and entourage at Galluis in 1936.* ABOVE: *Ganna Walska in the Callot-designed black velvet "Venus" gown, which she purchased while mourning for Dr. Franekel and continued to wear for sixteen years. The gown is now in the textiles collection of the Los Angeles County Museum of Art.*

THE 1930S
RESTLESSNESS AND
RESOLUTIONS
HARRY
GRINDELL-MATTHEWS

Harry Grindell-Matthews with eye patch (TOP), and after his operation in 1938.

which she finally recognized as "a mental and physical disturbance." With this new awareness, she "slowly but surely stopped leading a so-called social life." She gave up her extravagant parties at Galluis with entertainment such as the Isadora Duncan dancers on the lawn, with champagne in crystal glasses, and imported caviar served on antique china. Further, she no longer needed a man in order to feel complete: "…no more waiting for Prince Charming!"

Then, in June 1937, she met Harry Grindell-Matthews. Introduced by a mutual friend, they discovered a shared love for opera but had little else in common. He was a physicist and inventor who had coordinated sound with film before 1920, but was never credited with the invention of "talkies." He also had developed a wireless telephone, enabling airplane-to-ground communication and the remote control of airships and torpedoes. Newspaper stories often referred to him as "the inventor of the Death Ray," an experimental device that could disable car engines by remote control. His current project, carried on in a secret Welsh laboratory, was said to be an invention to deter air raids, and thus save the world from war.

Grindell-Matthews saw Ganna as the woman of his dreams, but the feeling was not mutual. She found him to be egotistical, jealous of the success of others, and emotionally unstable. He was also physically unattractive to her; he appeared haggard and untidy, was a chain smoker, and wore a patch over one eye that had been damaged in an experiment. When he asked her to marry him she responded that she would never marry again. He became so depressed by her rejection that he could not work. Mutual friends, and even government officials, begged her to marry him,

> *as it was feared that my indifference might kill him before his invention for detecting submarines and defending London against bombardment through rocket shooting could reach the hands of the War Ministry.*

Still she put him off, waiting for a portentous sign. The sign came when he had an operation to save the remaining sight in his good eye, and he recovered sight in both eyes. Seeing this outcome as nothing short of miraculous, she concluded:

> *I must consider it as a divine privilege to save this man for God's work! I hesitated no more …. I decided to marry him ….*

She invited Grindell-Matthews to recuperate from the operation at Galluis, where they discovered another characteristic they had in common–neither could bear to see broken branches in a tree. Perhaps the high point in their relationship was the gratitude Ganna felt when he pruned the dead wood from the trees at her château. Their engagement was announced in August 1937, allowing sufficient time for attorneys to prepare a pre-nuptial agreement before a January wedding in London. She returned to France immediately after the wedding, and he went back to work–he could not take the time for a honeymoon. Having accomplished her mission, enabling him to return to work, she still was bothered by his egotism, jealousy, and inappropriate social aspirations. Finally she concluded that "his small soul could not fulfill the "Divine Mission" of saving humanity from the wars …." The impending war provided a good excuse for her to return to America, and she escaped France on the last commercial clipper plane before the German occupation in 1940. She learned of Grindell-Matthews' death of a heart attack on September 11, 1941 via telegram from his housekeeper.

M ADAME WALSKA had not expected to return to "Inspirational America" until she was prepared for another concert tour.

> *For the second time in my life leaving Europe for America during a fratricidal war … I felt free again and more than ever before I breathed easier.*

Back in New York, she felt lost at first without the daily routine of voice lessons. Once she found a vocal teacher, she regained her inner serenity, but lost confidence in

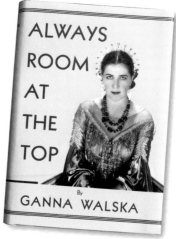

1940–1946

NEW YORK & CALIFORNIA, ANOTHER TRANSITION – THEOS BERNARD

her singing ability. In order to maintain her positive equilibrium and to share the lessons learned from her extraordinary life, she began writing her memoir, *Always Room at the Top.* It was at this point in her life that she met Theos Bernard. Toward the end of her book, she described him as an "American boy," who

> *unfolded to my soul so much the 'Real Knowledge of Divine Law' that I have stored up in my inner being enough food to digest and assimilate for the rest of this earthly life.*

Little could she imagine how indigestible that "food" would turn out to be. Madame Walska first encountered Theos Bernard in New York in 1940, when a friend invited her to attend Bernard's lecture and a yoga demonstration in Bernard's studio suite at the Hotel Pierre. The friend also loaned her Bernard's book, *The Penthouse of the Gods,* about the experiences in Tibet that earned him the title "The White Lama." Ganna was not impressed by Bernard, but signed on for daily yoga lessons at his center as a form of exercise and weight control. After several weeks she was invited to join Mr. Bernard's Wednesday evening seminars. Always seeking enlightenment, she accepted, but found Bernard an uninspiring teacher.

Private sessions were also frustrating because he refused to answer her questions, either about oriental philosophy or about himself. Through the course of the winter, however, she gradually came to understand that the Truth she sought was to come from within herself.

In the spring, Bernard made a social call and, to her amazement, declared that he had fallen in love with her the first time she attended his lecture. Further, he wanted to marry her the next day because it was the full moon. When she informed him that she was already married, he became furious and demanded that she ask for a divorce. Later, when she deflected his good-night kiss, he broke down and cried. That act did make an impression:

> *No wonder that my womanly, always motherly heart went out to this poor boy... I was sorry I did not suspect his agony and pushed him away so cruelly ...*

She did not know exactly what was troubling him, but she was certain that he was miserable, and that "I must help him because I am the stronger one. Thereupon our association started …"

Before long, Bernard began speaking enthusiastically of the natural beauty of

A portrait of Theos Bernard (top), *and a photo of Bernard in yoga position, taken from his book,* Hatha Yoga, *published in 1944 and dedicated to Ganna Walska.*

California, a place similar to India and Tibet, where he felt near to God. When her voice teacher announced that she was planning a trip to Hollywood, Ganna decided to go too, so as not to interrupt her lessons. She invited Bernard to go along. While she stayed in a tiny cottage in the Hollywood Hills, she rented a larger house and a car for Mr. Bernard.

Back in New York, by early 1941 Madame Walska began to be concerned about the state of the US economy under threat of war. More to the point, she was concerned about the security of her own finances. She had seen Polish and Russian aristocrats reduced to a life of poverty during the first World War. Having left France just ahead of the German occupation, she couldn't be sure that her French properties would ever be returned to her. She felt that the best way to safeguard against financial disaster would be to own a small self-sustaining ranch or farm. There, if necessary, she could retire to a simple life "independent of all servants." Influenced by Theos Bernard's enthusiasm and six glorious weeks in Hollywood, she felt that California would be the ideal location.

Theos Bernard, who had plans of his own, was more than happy to help locate her retreat. His ideal retreat would provide accommodations for Tibetan Lamas who would come to translate their holy works into English, as well as space for a Tibetan temple, a library, and a museum to house Madame Walska's extensive collection of Tibetan art. He flew to California to look at prospective properties. When he found Cuesta Linda he declared it "the perfect place" and insisted that she come see it immediately. She did as he demanded, but instead of the simple farm that she expected, she found:

> a white elephant—big estate with Italian gardens with two enormous swimming pools ... and which house alone certainly was looking far, far from a farmer's house I expected to see.

That same day he also took her to see the mountain-top estate that George Owen Knapp had named El Capitan when he built it in 1935. She was terrified by the

mountain road and despised the estate's ostentatious luxury in the midst of an awesome wilderness. Keenly aware that both properties would require tremendous sums of money for maintenance, but overwhelmed by Bernard's enthusiasm, she accepted his assertion that this was the destined place for the execution of his sacred work. She bought Cuesta Linda in June and El Capitan in September of 1941. As she put it:

> But what was the value of money when finally I found a companion with whom I could plan the future life according to my heart's desire, with an eye on my spiritual development. Here was lying my long-life craving. For the first time I could associate my earthy [sic] existence with one whose dreams were parallel of mine, who was looking for God and enlightenment.

In honor of its intended use, she and Bernard coined the name Tibetland for her new estate. Lofty El Capitan became Bernard's Penthouse of the Gods, a reference to his book on Tibet.

Reflecting back on this occasion later, painfully aware by then just how far from parallel Bernard's dreams had been from her own, she wrote:

> My whole life I ardently desired to live in a small house well hidden among protective trees ... I wished a garden tiny enough to count only on Nature's help for growing and blooming not being dependant on army of gardeners and landscapers, big enough however to nourish my body with nuts and fruit and my spirit with flowers and buds!

Tibetland was far from her dream retreat. She was not quite ready for total retreat, anyway, since being in New York for the opera season was still important to her. But she accepted the responsibility for management of the large estate (she left the Penthouse of the Gods to Bernard, except for paying the bills). It did seem a good place to spend summers away from the New York City heat and humidity, and she

was fascinated by the variety of tropical and desert plants that would grow there. She fulfilled her dream in one sense by taking the three-room pavilion attached to the main house as her "small house."

With America's entrance into the war and the State Department's blockage of visas from the orient, the Lamas were unable to come to Tibetland. At the end of the summer, when Ganna was ready to return to New York, Bernard decided that the best way to spend his time while waiting for the Lamas would be to complete his Ph.D. in Philosophy at Columbia University. She financed his educational expenses including private lessons in Sanskrit and other languages. In addition, she turned one level of her four-story house into a separate dwelling for him and, despite misgivings about strangers in her home, allowed him to conduct weekly public lectures there. Accepting of Bernard's self-centered attitude, she felt that if she indulged even his foolish desires, he would gain wisdom by seeing the error of his ways, and become worthy of her gifts. She had more difficulty dealing with his periodic blind rages that came without provocation or warning, but when spent, left

him sweet and childlike. Believing his violent mood swings were attributable to the loss of his mother at an early age, she vowed to take his mother's place, forgiving and caring for him as a mother surely would. With their twenty-year age gap, she was, in fact, of his mother's generation.

After Grindell-Matthews died, Bernard again began pressuring Madame Walska for marriage. He expressed fear that she would send him away, or her family and lawyers would remove him after her death. The assurance that she had willed both California properties to him didn't quell his insecurity. Seeing that the issue was interfering with his work, she finally agreed to marry him. Her attorney arranged for a secret ceremony in Las Vegas on July 27, 1942, but only after both parties signed a pre-nuptial agreement protecting her property in case of divorce.

The security of marriage did not transform Theos Bernard into a loving, generous person. Still, Madame Walska continued to financially support both Theos and his father, whom Bernard had originally introduced to her as his "friend," Mr. LaVarnie. Against her better judgment, she paid for the publication of his thesis,

A postcard view of the swimming pool at Cuesta Linda as it may have appeared when purchased by Ganna Walska in 1941.

ABOVE: *A gilded-bronze figure of Yama from Ganna Walska's extensive Tibetan art collection.*
RIGHT: *A postcard view of the house at* Cuesta Linda *before the addition of the pavilion.*
OPPOSITE: *The entrance at Sycamore Canyon Road is flanked by Chilean wine palms* (Jubaea chilensis) *and rows of* Agave franzosinii. *The iron gate was added by Madame Walska in 1946.*

Hatha Yoga. Her saintly attitude began to deteriorate in 1945. Bernard had gone to California in the fall, but she remained in New York. She planned to join him at Christmas, but changed her mind. During a stretch of severe winter weather and a series of minor illnesses, Ganna had plenty of time to think, eventually reaching the conclusion that: "I could not help him any longer without obscuring my own soul..." She wrote him long letters urging him to economize, pointing out his shortcomings, and trying to convince him that he was mentally ill. He responded by begging her to come to California for Easter. She finally made plane reservations for May 29, and Bernard was to meet her at the Burbank airport. Instead, she was greeted by a stranger who served her with divorce papers. When she comprehended the situation, Ganna was vastly relieved–until she arrived at Tibetland to discover that Bernard had removed many valuable furnishings and books from the house, including some of her favorite Tibetan pieces.

Bernard had sued for separate maintenance, claiming that he had been so spoiled by the life she provided him he was no longer able to support himself. Then it was revealed that he had been divorced in 1938 from another wealthy wife who had financed his early education and the two-year excursion to Tibet. The legal wrangling ended abruptly when he was caught committing perjury regarding his financial situation. Writing about the relationship in an unpublished manuscript she called *My Life With Yogi*, Madame Walska concluded:

> *Miraculously, almost in a twinkle of an eye I was vindicated. I got rid forever from such a dreadful individual without even any financial cost... I did not need any longer to care for him, not because I did not want to but because he himself gave me that unexpected undreamed of Freedom!*

Madame Walska demonstrated her freedom from Bernard's influence by renaming her estate Lotusland after the abundant flowers that remained in the original lotus pond. With her extensive exploration of Eastern religions, Madame Walska surely recognized the aptness of the lotus as a symbol of renewal and spiritual growth at this juncture of her life.

CHAPTER TWO

Lotusland –
Before Madame
Ganna Walska

THE PROPERTY THAT IS NOW known as Ganna Walska Lotusland had only two previous owners who made significant changes to the landscape before the arrival of Madame Walska. The original ninety-eight-acre parcel had been deeded by a homestead grant in 1877, and changed ownership five times in the next five years. Ralph Kinton Stevens (known simply as Kinton Stevens) was the first to make a permanent imprint upon the land. Born in Hertfordshire, England on January 30,1849, Stevens had been educated at King's College in London before he emigrated to Santa Barbara about 1873. He worked as a ranch hand and on a survey crew before his marriage to Caroline Lucy Tallant in 1881. In 1882 they settled on the property she named Tanglewood because of the dense growth of live oak trees and chaparral. The union produced three children: Ralph Tallant in 1882, Kinton Burkill in 1884, and Barbara Caroline in 1888.

Stevens' first challenge was to obtain a sufficient water supply for the lemon and palm nursery he intended to establish.

The well on the property was pumped by a windmill that could not produce a flow fast enough for direct irrigation, so he built a concrete reservoir at the highest location on the property. Once the reservoir was filled by the well water, gravity delivered the water as needed. Later he utilized a number of ingenious methods to maintain a steady water supply for his tropical plants. Even though he reduced his acreage, selling more than half of his property, the water available was never sufficient through the long dry season. Finally, Stevens created his own reservoir to collect winter rainfall by building an earthen dam across the low end of a swale in his hay field. To the delight of his children, he enhanced its appearance by creating a "tropical" island covered with bamboo and surrounded by Indian lotus, which eventually filled the pond.

Stevens became close friends with other local plantsmen, among them Dr. Francesco Franceschi, who initiated the Southern California Acclimatizing Association, and Dr. A. B. Doremus, who tested and planted many street trees in Santa Barbara. Stevens

TANGLEWOOD &
THE RALPH KINTON
STEVENS LEGACY

ABOVE LEFT: *The sandstone and shingle house built by Kinton Stevens in 1893.*
OPPOSITE: *The Olive Allée at Cuesta Linda in 1929.*

TOP: *The Monterey cypress that Kinton Stevens planted over 100 years ago towered over the garden in this 1950s photo of Belle Stevens and Ann Klein Stevens.*
ABOVE: *Pages from Kinton Stevens' 1893 nursery catalog.*
ABOVE RIGHT: *An early view of the valley in which Lotusland lies today.*

enjoyed entertaining the officers of trading vessels that docked in Santa Barbara, not only because he was a gregarious man, but also because they reciprocated his hospitality by sending him seeds and cuttings from around the world. Stevens' lemon nursery prospered, providing trees for many of the lemon orchards in the Santa Barbara area during the planting peak between 1886-1893. He had enough palms and other decorative exotic plants available by 1893 to publish the first nursery catalog in California devoted entirely to tropical and subtropical plants, according to garden historian Victoria Padilla. A display garden of rare plants around his own house demonstrated their potential as landscape plants and made his garden a local showplace. Large photographs of it were displayed at the 1894 midwinter World's Fair in San Francisco's Golden Gate Park. A rare South African silver tree that Stevens sent to the Chicago World's Fair in 1893 also created favorable publicity.

Although Stevens was not trained as a garden designer, many of his venerable specimens remain as dominant features in the garden. There was a Monterey cypress that commanded the attention from all viewpoints on the main lawn that was initially grown in a lath house. It was a favorite climbing tree for the Stevens children, whose activity may have assisted

the tree in destroying the lath house roof as it grew. The rippled gray surface of the Chilean wine palm trunks form repeated accents throughout the garden, especially in the Blue Garden and the Aloe Garden. The Dracaena Circle across the auto courtyard from the main house still encompasses part of Stevens' display garden, notably the oldest of the dragon trees, the large Canary Island date palms and more Chilean wine palms. Stevens' reservoir is now the heart of the Japanese Garden, although the current island is not the one Stevens created.

Kinton Stevens died of a heart attack in September 1896, at the age of 47. His widow remained on the property, struggling to maintain her family as she operated a guest ranch, then leased the property to a school. Finally, after both sons were in college, she moved with her daughter into a smaller house on the property and rented the large house to winter visitors. In 1913, she sold the property to George Owen Knapp, who had just finished building a house on his Arcady estate across Sycamore Canyon Road.

LIKE SO MANY OTHER early Montecito estate owners, Erastus Palmer Gavit came to California to escape eastern winters. Mr. Gavit's wealth came from the development of gas plants and electric traction companies, Albany, New York

businesses he had entered with his first father-in-law. Widowed and remarried, he first came to Santa Barbara with his daughter, Marcia Ann, and his new wife Marie in March 1915. He purchased the former Kinton Stevens estate from Knapp that same year. The family renamed the estate *Cuesta Linda*, Spanish for "pretty hill."

In keeping with the new estate name, the Gavits demolished the Stevens' native sandstone and shingle house, and hired Pasadena architect Reginald Johnson to design a Mediterranean style villa, as well as separate garage and studio buildings. In addition to its living room, small office, library, dining room, kitchen with butler's pantry and large work room, the house had six bedrooms and four bathrooms for family and guests, and another five bedrooms and two bathrooms in the servants' quarters.

The living room was dropped two steps below the main level, and the dining room featured a coffered ceiling; fireplaces graced six of the rooms. Other than a large carved stone decoration over the main entrance, the house exterior presented the pure lines and somewhat austere facade characteristic of Johnson's style. Renowned for his Spanish-influenced houses, Johnson received a gold medal for primacy in domestic architecture at the 1921 AIA Architectural Exhibit in Washington, D.C.

While the house was being designed, the Gavits hired Peter Riedel to renovate the neglected Stevens garden. He was assisted by Kinton Stevens' son, Ralph, who had received a degree in landscape design from Michigan State University, and had taught for five years at the University of California, Berkeley before returning to Santa Barbara

1916–1939
Cuesta Linda &
The Gavit Era

ABOVE: *An aerial view of the* Cuesta Linda *estate about 1920, showing the new house, the partially completed formal gardens, and the crescent-shaped pool and pathways which remain in the present Aloe Garden.*

TOP: *The Pavilion and patio, designed by George Washington Smith in 1925. Note the staircase descending from the house balcony to the Pavilion arcade.*
ABOVE: *Detail of the iron grillwork, also designed by Smith, that separates the patio from the main lawn.*

in 1917 as the first paid Superintendent of City Parks. Riedel had worked with Dr. Franceschi in the Southern California Acclimatizing Association. Both men were capable designers and knowledgeable about plants, but it is not known whether they made substantial changes to the garden or merely tidied up the existing plantings.

After the house was completed in February 1920, Paul Thiene was contracted to plan the formal gardens that remain behind the house. Thiene had been trained as a garden designer in his native Germany, but after working as head gardener of the 1915 San Diego Panama-California Exposition grounds, he decided to become a specialist in Spanish and Italian gardens. The formal garden that Thiene designed for the Gavits is arranged in traditional Italianate style, with brick paths intersecting at right angles, changing levels, water features, and tall hedges providing a sense of mystery and enclosure. Unlike most Italianate estate gardens, however, the major axis is not approached directly from the living areas of the house, but rather from a walled and balustraded terrace separate from the house. Early photographs indicate that this axis, with its Moorish fountain, was completed later; thus, it may not have been part of Thiene's design. The axis that contains the Neptune fountain, viewed from the dining room and its terrace, may have been Thiene's primary axis. A third long axis marks the

transition between the formal and informal portions of the garden: a straight brick path along the edge of the citrus orchard, extending into a wider allée of olive trees. The central cross-axis continues into the citrus orchard as a lemon-covered arbor.

The Gavits made several additions to the estate during the 1920s. For these projects, they called upon George Washington Smith, a Santa Barbara architect. Smith had studied architecture at Harvard, but left without earning a degree and became a stockbroker in order to make a better living. Once he had accrued sufficient money, he was able to study architecture by traveling in Europe, and finally return to his first love, designing country houses. His first project, a house for himself in Montecito, received enough favorable attention to begin attracting clients.

It was probably soon after the Gavits moved into the house that Smith was engaged to surround the estate with a wall. In 1924 he designed the stable (later converted to a music studio by Madame Walska). In 1925 the Gavits asked him to design a separate Pavilion for their daughter. The original plans show three bedrooms, each with its own bath/dressing room and two separate entrances into the large patio that separated the Pavilion from the main house. The patio was accessible from the main house by stairs both from the library on the main level and the second-floor balcony above it. Enclosure was completed by a solid wall on the driveway side and by three arches with wrought iron fencing and gate opening to the lawn. The octagonal fountain in the patio bears striking similarities to the eight-pointed Moorish fountain that is the centerpiece of the formal garden below the house. Both use colorful tiles and play on the movement and sound of water trickling along narrow runnels, and in both designs, the water was then carried out into the lawn by means of underground pipes. Smith's work exhibited a more colorful, Spanish-Moorish approach to design than Johnson's Italianate style, as displayed in the variety of tiles used to crown each column of the arcade along the length of the building, the interaction of the two stairways from the house, and the

wrought iron pattern, resembling filigree work. Comparing the known Smith work to the Moorish fountain and walled terrace in the main formal garden, it seems reasonable to attribute the latter projects to Smith rather than to Theine.

Smith's final major project for the Gavits was to design the original swimming pool and bath house. There, his imagination took flight as he conceptualized a rectangular pool flanked by two semi-circular lily ponds. Swimming in the pool, one could imagine oneself in a natural, lily-filled pond. The three-room bath house displays arches similar to those used in the Pavilion arcade, as well as more of Smith's characteristic tile work. A long axis bisects the pool, from steps above the tiled benches at the northern end through a path that extended southward between a double row of Italian cypress to a distant "wishing well." From that point, water stairs flowed down into Kinton Stevens' lotus pond, which was reduced in size and made more picturesque in shape. The water stairs were designed by Peter Riedel, the Dutch horticulturist, with Smith as a consultant.

The Gavits' gardens were constructed within the foundation of Kinton Stevens' famed plant collection and demonstration garden. With the additions made by the Gavits, *Cuesta Linda* gained a reputation as one of the finer estates in Montecito. From 1926 onward, it was always included in the summer "Garden Tour" fundraisers for the Santa Barbara Plans and Planting Committee. When Presidential candidate Herbert Hoover made a half-day campaign stop in Santa Barbara in August 1928, Cuesta Linda was one of the four estates he visited.

Marie Gavit died in 1937, having been preceded in death by her husband. The estate was sold to Sir Humphrey Clarke, a British diplomat, in 1939. The Clarkes are not known to have made any changes to the landscape, although they did alter the interior of the house by adding Italian marble mantle pieces and an ornate French banister, and further compromised the Mediterranean design by squaring off several arched doorways.

CHAPTER THREE

Evolution of the Gardens at Lotusland

WHEN MADAME WALSKA purchased Tibetland in 1941, she hired the best-known landscape architect in Santa Barbara, Lockwood de Forest, to help renovate the neglected grounds. Although de Forest had considerable fame as a landscape architect, his role for her encompassed more than design. During the two years of their working relationship he selected fruit trees and oversaw the installation of an entirely new orchard, supervised the repair of the glasshouse and greenhouse, and directed soil fungus treatments to save the lives of oak and cypress trees. One of his bills is for "setting statues purchased from the Ludington estate." These may be the ones in the original succulent garden, which de Forest planted. At her request, he also planned and planted gardens around the Rose Cottage, the Green Cottage, the garage, and the stable when it was converted into her music studio.

An indication that there were both similarities to and differences from the Lotusland of today can be found in the garden areas mentioned in de Forest's bills.

His notes referred to: a swimming pool, lotus pond, formal garden, house garden, lower garden, fuchsia garden, rose garden, palm grove, bamboo, and cactus garden. There was also reference to a "garden of different cactus," a "rainbow pool," and "the jungle." A "silver garden and oasis" contained agave and dusty miller. The "blue garden" was planted with blue flowering plumbago, ceratostygma, lilies, and delphiniums.

During the summer of 1942 Madame Walska asked de Forest to seek out interesting and mature cactus to replace the traditional landscape treatment in front of the house. Many were dug from the nearby estate of John Wright. Neither Wright nor de Forest knew the scientific names of many of the specimens selected, so individual plants were billed by descriptions or sketches. The working relationship between Madame Walska and de Forest went beyond the usual designer-client relationship. Initially serving as teacher and advisor to a woman who had little horticultural knowledge but knew the visual effect she wanted to achieve, he soon became a willing collaborator in carrying out her ideas. Upon his departure to serve in the

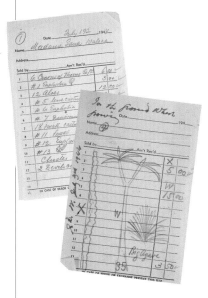

TOP: *Ganna Walska in the Blue Garden.* ABOVE: *John Wright's bills for cactus.* OPPOSITE: *The original swimming pool after conversion to a water garden, 1950s.*

TOP: *Weeping* Euphorbia ingens *in front of the main house.* ABOVE: *The swimming pool with South Pacific clamshells on its beach, designed by Ralph Stevens in 1947.* ABOVE, RIGHT: *Ganna Walska poses amid her cactus plantings in 1958.*

1943–1955
RALPH STEVENS

camouflage section of the army, de Forest wrote Madame Walska:

> *You are wonderful! I never would have thought of using cactus at the front door, or many of the other plantings you suggested. They are very handsome and I congratulate you.*

Such a compliment coming from a respected designer must have given Madame Walska great confidence when she contemplated her next garden addition.

WHEN MADAME WALSKA learned that Ralph Stevens, Superintendent of Parks for Santa Barbara, had been born and raised on her estate, she contacted him for advice. As busy as Stevens was with the city parks, he willingly found time for consultation at Lotusland. During the stormy Theos Bernard years, Stevens' work was primarily purchasing plants and supervising their installation, and designing some wooden planter boxes. Once the divorce was behind her, Madame Walska was ready to commence more significant projects. Security-conscious, she asked Stevens to design a gate for the Sycamore Canyon Road

entrance to the estate; it was manufactured by Craviotto Iron Works and installed in 1946.

After consulting with pool experts, Madame Walska concluded that converting the Gavits' swimming pool to meet contemporary standards was not feasible, and plans were made for a new swimming pool, seventy-five feet long, shaped like a stylized classic fountain. In 1947, Paddock Pools was contracted to construct the pool to Stevens' specifications. Stevens also designed the shell-strewn beach and the low sandstone wall that provides both planting pockets for succulents and a sense of enclosure to the area. Stonemason Oswald Da Ros constructed the wall.

The following summer, Madame Walska requested a grotto and a theatre garden, similar to those she had on the grounds of her château in Galluis. She had been able to retrieve some of her Galluis treasures after the war, including several antique carved stone figures from the theater garden there, and wished to place them in a similar setting. Stevens' design provided seating for a hundred on three tiers of sandstone benches, with hedges of Monterey cypress forming the walls and stage backdrop. Oswald Da Ros

did the stonework for both the grotto and the outdoor theater.

At the end of 1948, Stevens took the first step toward the creation of today's Blue Garden, ordering several blue Atlas cedars for the then-designated "Silver Garden." As Madame Walska acquired cactus by the truckload, he arranged groupings of cactus down the driveway. Stevens' final project for Madame Walska was to design a horticultural clock as a centerpiece for an extension of the formal garden, with beds designated for topiary. Of Stevens' design, only the clock, planted with succulents, was actually executed–in 1955. Whether Madame Walska rejected the formality of his design or simply became impatient to begin acquiring the topiary is not known, but by 1957 the area around her twenty-five-foot clock (reported by the *Santa Barbara News Press* at that time to be the "largest floral clock in the world") was filled with fanciful topiary animals acquired from Osaki Plant Zoo in Los Angeles.

Like Lockwood de Forest, Ralph Stevens also became an admirer of Madame Walska's unusual planting ideas. According to garden historian Victoria Padilla, Lotusland was his favorite of all the gardens he designed:

In it Stevens was able to display his talents to their utmost and in so doing produced one of the most notable gardens in the United States.

Although she always had trouble with horticultural nomenclature, Ganna Walska quickly absorbed the principles of designing with plants. Stevens gave credit to her contributions when he described Lotusland as being,

…typical of Madame Walska's feeling, her sense of theatrical and spectacular, rather than in the intimate interest of the plants themselves. She has an artist's feeling, using plants instead of paints for stage settings.

By the end of her first decade developing the gardens at Lotusland Madame Walska expressed great pride in having succeeded in creating,

from an abandoned to nature jungle… most beautiful showplace with tremendous variety of everything that the generous California climate could produce.

THE THEATRE GARDEN

ABOVE: *Several 'Grotesques,' antique stone figures came from Madame's estate in Galluis.* LEFT: *The Theatre Garden, restored by landscape architect Isabelle Greene in 1988. The original hedges of Monterey cypress had become overgrown with English ivy when Ganna Walska Lotusland Foundation took over in 1984. Greene selected African boxwood* (Myrsine Africana) *for the outer walls, and fern pine* (Podocarpus gracilior) *for the stage backdrop and wings, and changed the previous formal placement of some of the stone figures to a more playfully theatrical arrangement.*

EVENTS IN THE GARDEN

TOP: *Ganna Walska with actor Leo Carrillo at a Fiesta party in 1958.* ABOVE: *A Polish Easter party in 1951.* FROM LEFT: *Polish movie star Loda Halama, Mrs. Borodin, Ganna Walska, Hania Puacz.* RIGHT: *At a summer party in 1957, Ganna Walska entertains her brother Leon Puacz and his family.*

OPENING THE GARDEN
TO THE PUBLIC

She sang the praises of the theatrical allée of Italian cypresses, her *theatre de verdure*, and her "masterpiece" of a swimming pool with its stone wall and sandy beach. Her highest praise went to

> … *the monarch of all flowers, the unique lotus with its sacred blossoms from which we derived the name of Lotusland for our estate.*

In a letter to a friend, Madame Walska wrote in 1951,

> *The place, meaning the gardens, is out of this world! I kept working all summer and it certainly became the most valuable and rare collection of cacti, palms, agaves, etc.*

SOON AFTER she came to Lotusland, Madame Walska had been asked by Miss Pearl Chase, preservationist and Chair of the Santa Barbara Plans and Planting Committee, to continue Mrs. Gavit's tradition of opening the garden for the Annual Garden Tours. Except for a few summers when Madame Walska deemed that construction projects rendered the garden unsuitable for viewing, Lotusland was included in these benefit tours from 1943 through 1967. The garden lent itself so well

for entertaining, she generously sponsored other benefits, too; recipients included the American Women's Voluntary Services, Our Lady of Mount Carmel Church and, on several occasions, the Music Academy of the West. She freely opened the garden to garden clubs and educational groups, ranging from the Cold Spring School Brownie Troop to the students in Ornamental Horticulture at Cal Poly San Luis Obispo. Although she had forsworn elaborate parties during her last years at Galluis, Lotusland inspired her to play the role of hostess again. Favorite occasions were her Fiesta parties, held during Santa Barbara's annual Old Spanish Days celebration, with costumes, catered food, and pony cart rides for the children.

The social events were enjoyable, but when the Cactus and Succulent Society requested a tour during their biennial convention in 1953, she knew that Lotusland had developed a significance beyond mere space for entertaining. In the ensuing years, she was honored by several more visits from the Cactus and Succulent Society, as well as the Bromeliad Society and the Palm Society. These were tours for which the garden had to be in perfect condition!

The Horticultural Clock

ABOVE: *Madame Walska and the clock designed by Ralph Stevens, soon after its installation in 1955. The clock works were custom made by AdVance Time in St. Louis, Missouri. Copper zodiac signs were crafted by Gunnar Thielst, who closed his own ornamental ironwork studio to work with Madame Walska on many garden projects for over twenty-five years.*

LEFT: *Lotusland's original topiary animals from the Osaki Plant Zoo in Los Angeles, still in tubs before they were planted in the ground in 1957.*

Ganna Walska at work in her gardens, above and right.

1956–1973

MADAME GANNA
WALSKA, HEAD
GARDENER

AFTER RALPH STEVENS' retirement, Madame Walska could not find another suitable head gardener. Many were hired, but either they were fired within a few days or they quit because they found Madame Walska too difficult to please. In letters to friends she despaired that the garden would never be finished. But, just as she had continued singing after each poorly-received opera performance, so she mustered the strength to manage the day-to-day work of the garden. She did retain some capable and dedicated people on her garden staff. And she received valuable information and advice in correspondence with the plant collectors and growers who supplied her. One of them, cactus field collector Antonia Crowninshield, developed an eye for plants that would please Madame Walska and frequently delivered them in person, driving her truck all the way from Arizona. Mrs. Crowninshield supplied many of the golden barrel cactus, at Madame Walska's exuberant request:

> *Hooray for the golden barrels! Even though you don't write how big or how small they are ... I... want to have a monopoly for all barrels, grandfather, mother or babies.*

Madame Walska almost single-handedly managed the conversion of the old swimming pool into a water garden between 1953 and 1956, with the aid, via correspondence, of J. T Charleson of Tricker Water Gardens in Ohio. He, in turn, was so impressed by the photographs of her results that he asked permission to retain them for advertising purposes. Locally, she didn't hesitate to call upon the best, including E.O. Orpet, a well-known horticulturist and former Santa Barbara City Parks Superintendent who had established a cactus nursery in retirement.

In addition to being a first-rate stonemason, Oswald Da Ros obtained most of the stone that was added to the garden. He was willing to travel, to Mono Lake, San Diego County, or the beach at Dos Pueblos Ranch to hand-select just the right stones, occasionally accompanied by Madame Walska. Whenever he came across unusual or valuable stones or crystals, he bought them, knowing Madame Walska would probably want them. It was Da Ros who ordered from the Arrowhead Water Company the loads of blue slag glass that line so many of Lotusland's paths. He also proved to be a valuable resource for people who could help with special projects. When, in 1958, Madame Walska wanted to enhance the crescent-shaped pool in the Aloe Garden, Da Ros introduced her to artist Joseph Knowles, Sr., who helped arrange the abalone shells for the border and drew several sketches of fountains utilizing giant clam-shells for her selection. When she needed an aviary, Da Ros found Paul Linwall, a shipbuilder, to do the job. When she wanted a collection of scented pelargoniums on the house terrace, Da Ros introduced her to Jim Minah, a knowledgeable hobby grower. She was amazed to discover later that Minah was

CACTUS
AND
SUCCULENT JOURNAL
Of the Cactus And Succulent Society Of America

Vol. XXV   SEPT.-OCT., 1953   No. 5

FIG. 97. Madame Ganna Walska, Santa Barbara, Calif., has the largest private collection of cacti in America.

LEFT: *The 1953* Cactus and Succulent Journal *honored Ganna Walska on the cover and her Garden was described as "a cactophile's Eden."*

also an artist, and in 1969, engaged him to design the pebble mosaics below the dining room terrace.

SEVERAL MAJOR PROJECTS were accomplished during the 1960s. Madame Walska began a collection of bromeliads, purchasing most of them from Hummel's Exotic Gardens in Carlsbad and from Fritz Kubisch, an orchid grower and proprietor of Jungle Plants and Flowers in Culver City. In 1968 Kubisch was asked to arrange them in the shelter of a large live oak tree, creating the original Bromeliad Garden where it could be viewed from the Pavilion terrace.

FRITZ KUBISCH
THE BROMELIAD GARDEN

WILLIAM PAYLEN
THE FERN GARDEN

The pebble mosaic, above, was designed by Jim Minah and installed by Osawld Da Ros in 1969. When Da Ros could not find pebbles in all of the colors desired, he devised a method to shape his own by tumbling chunks of stone in a cement mixer. The Neptune fountain and surrounding tile walls were restored in 1996.

MADAME WALSKA had read an article about Bill Paylen's work in the *Fern Society Journal*, and invited him to come for a garden tour and to discuss a new fern garden. It was agreed that he would build the garden gradually, coming just one day a week. The first step would be to create a backdrop of large tufa stones that would define the perimeters of the garden and provide raised platforms on which mosses and small ferns would grow. When the load of stones was delivered, Madame Walska phoned Paylen to inform him that she did not like them. He responded simply, "Madame, you will like them." When he arrived the next week to study the stones and plan their arrangement, he found a crane and a crew of workers ready to set the stones. Aware of Madame Walska's aversion to machinery in the garden, he thought it best to begin with the largest stone. But before the crane could maneuver

the rock into place, it bogged down in the mud. To avoid a scene with Madame Walska, Paylen ordered the driver to drop the rock, and began his garden design from that point. After all the rocks were in place, plants were added gradually during his weekly visits between 1968 and 1972. They didn't always agree about details, but resolved their differences cordially. For example, Madame Walska resisted the inclusion of flowering plants until Paylen offered to supply a collection of rare and unusual begonias. Many were purchased from local begonia hybridizer Rudolph Ziesenhenne. At the end of the project, Paylen wrote in a letter to Madame Walska:

> *Madame, I could never have created the Fem Garden at Lotusland without your help and generosity. You gave me always a free hand and I am so grateful about that.*

ABOVE: *The Lower Bromeliad Garden, created by Charles Glass when the overcrowded bromeliads near the Pavilion were relocated to the area formerly called "the jungle." Later, William Paylen rearranged and expanded the plantings.*
LEFT: *The original Fern Garden, designed and planted by William Paylen between 1968 and 1972. He expanded the Fern Garden in 1986–1988.*

THE JAPANESE GARDEN was the most significant and time consuming accomplishment during the late 1960s. Madame Walska had begun by asking three different Japanese garden designers to submit plans. However, she couldn't interpret them, so she called on Oswald Da Ros for advice. He pointed out to her that she had a skilled Japanese gardener already on her staff– Frank Fujii, who had been hired to trim the topiaries. Fujii had previously worked with his father, Kintsuchi Fujii. The elder Fujii had trained as a garden designer in Japan, and had come to America in 1904; one of his jobs had been to help create the Japanese Garden in San Francisco's Golden Gate Park.

Thus was formed an unusual but effective design team: Frank Fujii had learned Japanese gardening concepts from his father; Oswald Da Ros knew how to manipulate rocks into place so they would look as if they were meant to be there; and Madame Walska knew what she liked (if only after she had seen it in place). Her first request was for a cycad island in the pond. To reduce the chances of having to repeat a difficult task requiring a barge and crane, Da Ros asked Jim Minah to draw the proposed island, then, after Madame Walska's approval, built it to exactly match the drawing. The work did not always go smoothly. Construction of the waterfall took a long time, and the truck and crane blocked Madame Walska's view of the progress. Finally, she became impatient and made them move the truck (a slow and tricky procedure in such a tight space) so that she could get a good look. Then the first granite slab brought in to bridge the water flowing from the waterfall into the pond was deemed

THE JAPANESE GARDEN

OPPOSITE: *The Torii Gathering and Arch Bridge in the renovated Japanese Garden overlook serene and contemplative settings at the water's edge.*

ABOVE: *The pond in the Japanese Garden attracts a variety of wild birds, including snowy and great egrets, green and great blue herons, wood ducks, black phoebes, and belted kingfishers. The Japanese Garden underwent an extensive renovation in 2018.*

ABOVE: *Clustering* Echeveria *in the succulent garden.* RIGHT: *View of Reginald Johnson designed Main House with massed golden barrel cacti* (Echinocactus grusonii) *in the foreground.*

1973–1983

CHARLES GLASS & ROBERT FOSTER

too small by Madame Walksa, and Da Ros had to obtain a larger one–no matter that it had to be trucked from San Diego County. When Madame Walska saw that the stone foundation for the Torii gate extended into the driveway, she insisted that Da Ros cut it to the edge of the driveway. This was one occasion when Da Ros refused to do her bidding, and after two weeks she thanked him for it.

C HARLES GLASS was editor of the *Cactus and Succulent Journal* in 1972 when he wrote a very favorable article describing a recent tour of Lotusland by the Cactus and Succulent Society. Glass and

Robert Foster were co-owners of Abbey Cactus Gardens and Abbey Garden Press, located at that time in Reseda. After she read the article Madame Walska began calling Glass, asking him and Foster to come work with her at Lotusland. They refused, but each time she bought plants from their nursery she asked them to supervise the installation, giving her opportunities to ask again and again. Finally, they were convinced that if they didn't help with the establishment of her planned Lotusland Foundation, the garden might not survive after her death. They envisioned developing a teaching and research oriented botanic garden, and saw

in Lotusland a worthy setting for their own enormous collection of cacti and succulents.

Glass and Foster began garden renovations in 1973 with the original Succulent Garden and continued the following year with the driveway plantings. In each case, all the plants were removed, the soil was amended and mounded for better drainage, lava rocks and pitted San Felipe stone were added to contrast with the plants, and the beds were mulched with lava rock to great dramatic effect. By 1975 they were ready to tackle the Aloe Garden in the same manner, but with even more pronounced topography, raising the soil level as much as seven feet in some places. However, there was no truck access into the area and Madame Walska adamantly refused permission to create a temporary roadway.

Determined to proceed with their plan, they resorted to wheelbarrows, and moved the large stones with rollers and levers. With many aloes from their own collection added to Madame Walska's, the completed garden contained over one hundred different species.

After all of the succulents had been replanted, Bob Foster resigned from Lotusland to devote his full time to the Abbey Garden Press. Charles Glass stayed on to accomplish his most satisfying Lotusland project, the Cycad Garden. Madame Walska had an impressive collection of cycads, some purchased as early as the 1950s. They were growing among the sandstone concretions near the Theatre Garden, where they were too crowded for a good display and too shaded for healthy growth. In the fall of 1975

The sun highlights old man cactus (Cephalocereus senilis) *and* Notocacus leninghausii *near the driveway.*

Glass approached Madame Walska with a proposal to create a new Cycad Garden in a neglected area that had been Kinton Stevens' grain field. Placement of the three rare *Encephalartos woodii* turned out to be the only hindrance to total agreement between Madame Walska and Glass. His idea was to feature them at the garden's entrance, but she wanted visitors to have the delightful experience of "discovering" them. Once they had agreed to place them well into the garden, on a rocky cliff above their own koi pond, work could begin. In 1977, after two years of earth moving and path laying, the site was ready to begin placing some five hundred cycads. Sometimes called a "million dollar garden" because its development coincided with the well-publicized auction of Madame WaIska's enormous jewelry collection, which earned nearly that amount, the completed Cycad Garden "opened" during a special tour to benefit the Santa Barbara Botanic Garden in August 1979. Pleased with the results, Glass told Madame Walska, " ... this will be one of the greatest achievements of our lives." Glass was not exaggerating. With over two hundred species represented, the Lotusland cycad collection was second to only one other in the world– the public *Orto Botanico* garden near Naples, Italy. A decade later, Glass reminisced over his pride and pleasure in the creation of the Cycad Garden, "How few people could ever have the chance to landscape on that scale and with such a fabulous collection of rare, virtually irreplaceable plants!"

ABOVE: *The brick pathways in the Aloe Garden date from the Gavit era.* OPPOSITE: *Aloe lutescens, A. marlothii, and A. speciosa, three of more than 160 species featured in the Aloe Garden.*

ABOVE: *In the Cycad Garden, three rare* Encephalartos woodii *thrive above a koi filled pond, in a setting designed by Charles Glass. Once believed to be extinct, all the known E. woodii in the world derive from a single specimen discovered in South Africa in 1902 and planted in the Durban Botanic Garden in 1904.* RIGHT: *The Blue Garden was renovated in 2012 to admit more sunlight to the garden. The understory plants were replanted to re-create the original cool color palette.*

ABOVE: *The Dracaena Circle, across from the Main House, retains some of the plantings from the Kinton Stevens' demonstration garden. Madame Walska was so fond of the dragon trees (Dracaena draco) that she created a virtual forest of them by transplanting large specimens. Left: Ganna Walska converted a crescent-shape pool from the Gavit era into her abalone shell pond in the Aloe Garden, with fountains crafted from giant South Pacific clamshells.*

ABOVE: *Madame Walska in 1957 at her niece, Hania Tallmadge's wedding. She always wore the two medals she received, one the Polish Cross of Merit, the other from the French government.*
RIGHT: *The Main House now serves as offices for the public charity, Ganna Walska Lotusland.*

MADAME WALSKA
AS BENEFACTOR

Many local organizations benefited from Madame Walska's generosity, including: the Music Academy of the West (with financial contributions as well as donations of costumes); the Lobero Theatre; the Santa Barbara Symphony; the Santa Barbara Museum of Art (for a painting by Marc Chagall); Santa Barbara Beautiful (for pruning of dead fronds from palm trees along Cabrillo Boulevard); and the Community Arts Music Association (to sponsor a special performance of the Polish National Radio Orchestra).

I N HER LATER YEARS, Madame Walska's arthritis made walking painful, but the desire to keep abreast of ongoing projects prompted daily walks, eventually with the aid of two canes. The completion of the Cycad Garden may have reduced her motivation to get out into the garden, but she remained reluctant to permit even routine tasks such as pruning without her personal supervision. Some areas, such as the topiaries, suffered irreversible damage during this period of delayed maintenance. A broken hip in 1982 left her bed-ridden the last months of her life. When the end came, March 2, 1984, the Ganna Walska Lotusland Foundation, which she had conceived in 1958, assumed ownership and operation of the garden.

Lotusland is a wondrous and generous gift to the world from Madame Walska, but in the end, she probably would have agreed that she gained from it as much as she gave. Primarily, it provided an outlet for her prodigious creative energy. As she focused her attention on each garden area, she was never bored, and she never stopped learning, becoming familiar with the vocabulary, cultural requirements, and aesthetic qualities of each plant group as they were manipulated

into the compositions of her imagination. The garden also brought her the respect and recognition that she had sought, but failed to find, on the opera stage. When the members of the Cactus and Succulent Society came to study her work, when Pearl Chase wrote annually to request that she open the garden for the benefit tour, when entertaining became a performance with the entire garden as her stage—all of the many occasions that brought admiration for her creation must have given her as much satisfaction as a hundred curtain calls. And, finally, in her garden she found resolution to many of the questions that had prompted her relentless quest for spiritual and religious guidance throughout her life. At long last, she found spiritual peace.

After Madame Walska's death in 1984, five Trustees were appointed to the Ganna Walska Lotusland Foundation. The newly created Board was guided by the wish expressed in Madame Walska's will " ... to develop Lotusland to its maximum capacity into the most outstanding center of horticultural significance and of educational use." In preparation for public tours of the garden, deferred maintenance was performed, paths were repaired, and handicap access was improved. With an expanded staff and the establishment of a docent program, the goals were accomplished. A Conditional Use Permit to open the garden was granted by the Santa Barbara County Planning Commission in 1992.

The Visitor Center with its entrance gate on Cold Springs Road was completed in time for the first scheduled tour on September 15, 1993. The building's arches were modeled after the 1920s George Washington Smith Bathhouse. In keeping with Madame Walska's penchant for themed gardens, an Australian Garden was deemed appropriate within the old eucalyptus grove. Sydney Baumgartner was responsible for the design, massing various myrtles, grevilleas, and acacias to screen the parking area, and placing some more unusual specimens, such as Anigozanthus, Doryanthes, and Xanthorrhoea for dramatic effect. The arbor-covered walkway through which visitors enter the garden was planted with Australian tea trees.

By the time the garden was opened to the public, most of the topiary figures that had delighted children since the 1960s were beyond restoration. Only a few of the smaller and less elaborate figures remained in the garden, though some of the bare metal forms were left to show visitors the scale of Madame Walska's plant menagerie. Fortunately, one of Lotusland's docents designed and created topiaries professionally. Lori Ann David was not only capable, but also very interested in restoring the Topiary Garden. Volunteering her time, she researched Madame Walska's original topiaries, drew a plan based on Ralph Stevens' unrealized design, and re-created four of the original frames for display during a fundraising gala, in the hope that public enthusiasm would stimulate

1984–1993

PREPARATIONS FOR PUBLIC OPENING

1995–2001

TOPIARY GARDEN

ABOVE: *Inspired by Ralph Stevens' plan, the new Topiary Garden is divided into quadrants by new brick walkways that also encircle the restored horticultural clock.*

47

support. In the year 2000, a campaign was initiated as a tribute to Carol Valentine, President of the Board since 1989, who had advocated restoration of the Topiary Garden. Most of the figures designed by Lori Ann David replicate the originals. She drew on her creative imagination to enliven other creatures with innovative plant combinations, such as the blue-flowering Hardenbergia "Happy Wanderer" used for the peacock's tail.

IN 1998, after more than thirty apparently healthy cycads had died of fungal infections and root rot, the horticultural staff initiated a five-year plan to remedy the situation. In consultation with cycad experts it was determined that the best solution would be to remove all the infected soil and install a drainage system beneath new sandy topsoil. A cold frame with bottom-heated pumice beds was constructed as a nursery for the first forty-eight plants, which had undergone fungicide treatment after being lifted. In 2000, the first cycads were replanted and a second smaller batch was transferred to the greenhouse while their area was improved. Some eucalyptus trees and fan palms were removed to reduce competition for water, nutrients, and light. During the following two years, the Cycad Garden was

extended to provide space for Lotusland's growing cycad collection. Bamboo was planted to screen the garden from adjacent roads, and insectaries were planted to attract beneficial insects. As the healthy cycads were replanted, compatible accent plants and sandstone boulders were added to enhance the beds, and the paths were graded and graveled to be wheelchair accessible. Now thriving, the garden proudly reasserts its position among the finest cycad collections in the world.

MADAME WALSKA's cactus collection was lauded in a 1952 issue of the *Cactus and Succulent Journal* as "one of the outstanding cactus gardens of the West." Thereafter, the Cactus and Succulent Society scheduled several visits, during which it was admired by hundreds of cactus growers. One such admirer was Merritt S. Dunlap of Glendale, whose own cactus collection then included over one thousand species and varieties. Concerned about the future of his collection, in 1966 Dunlap offered to bequeath it to Madame Walska and she accepted. Dunlap continued to expand his collection for thirty-five more years, and moved it to his new home in San Diego County during the 1970s. Dunlap reiterated his concern for the collection in 1989, as

his age and arthritis were making garden work difficult. During the 1990s, Lotusland horticultural staff began visiting Dunlap and scheduling workdays to help maintain the cacti. The contents of Dunlap's small greenhouse were moved to Lotusland early in 2000. During 2001, the remaining cacti were transported in twelve weekly trips with a stake-sided truck. To avoid damaging the larger specimens, wooden boxes were constructed around their partially excavated roots before lifting them; uprights on the boxes were secured to a framework built across the truck bed. Finally, the thirty-one largest cacti were loaded onto semi-trucks for the trip to Lotusland. A temporary nursery was created to hold the cacti at Lotusland until the new Cactus Garden was ready for installation.

Lotusland staff had selected the site and affirmed that the new garden had to be in keeping with Madame Walska's dramatic style. Surveying the works of several designers, they concluded that Eric Nagelmann shared Madame Walska's ability to surprise and delight visitors. A Santa Barbara native and long-time fan of Lotusland, Nagelmann generously donated his landscape design and consultation services, aware that the plants were under stressful conditions and that funds were not

yet available. A fund-raising campaign was initiated with a leadership gift by Trustee Michael Towbes. The campaign was very successful and a beautiful plaque at the entrance to the Cactus Garden recognizes the donors, with a special tribute to Merritt Dunlap. Construction of the garden began in February 2003 with 300 tons of basalt used to create planting beds and a central viewing mound. Plants are grouped by their country of origin, as they had been in Dunlap's garden, but there the similarity ends. Although the garden is completely open, its full scope is obvious only from the mounded viewing platform. At ground level, the impressive size of the cacti and basalt columns along the paths overwhelms the senses. The rugged "outcroppings" of basalt boulders and the dark slate used as a heat-reflecting mulch create a sense of a harsh, alien territory, suitable only for the toughest inhabitants–suitable indeed for this amazing cactus collection.

1996–2004
NEW CACTUS GARDEN

ABOVE: *The viewing mound in the Cactus Garden affords an overview of the impressive collection and a peek of the distant hills.*

ABOVE: *The fountain at the Visitor Center, designed by tile artist Judith Sutcliffe, features Lotusland's signature plant, the sacred lotus.* RIGHT: *In the Upper Bromeliad Garden, this striking juxtaposition of bromeliads, native to jungles, with cacti would be impossible to achieve in most environments.*

ABOVE: *A simple water staircase, designed by Dutch horticulturalist Peter Riedel with architect George Washington Smith as consultant, was built in the 1920s. A long brick walkway lined with Italian cypress connected it to the Water Garden and swimming pool. These features were renovated in 2009.*

CHAPTER FOUR

Lotusland Today

GANNA WALSKA Lotusland invites guests to experience the Garden as created, neither censuring its exuberance nor hiding its whimsy. By interpreting the amazing collections of rare and unusual plants amassed by Madame Walska, Lotusland is a tribute to the fragility of our world and the need to preserve its biodiversity. Through the generosity of its members and other benefactors, Lotusland has been able to restore early garden features long past their prime. They have also made it possible for Lotusland to provide work experience training and internships for students majoring in horticulture and botany. Members are invited to special classes, lectures, and field trips where they can broaden their knowledge of botany, horticulture, garden design, and conservation, both at home and abroad.

Environmental responsibility is valued at Lotusland, not only as appropriate for this garden, but also as a model for others. As exemplary stewards of the environment, the staff has adopted pesticide-free and sustainable techniques, maintaining plant health by organic methods. The soil is improved by utilizing compost and mulch derived from green waste. Beneficial insects, fostered in insectaries, devour harmful insects, and weeds are eliminated with old-fashioned manual techniques. With these methods, excessive fertilization and the use of toxic products can be avoided, benefiting both the Garden and its visitors.

Lotusland is supported by its endowments, membership program, admission fees, fundraising events, grants, and donations. A Wall of Honor erected near the Visitor Center lists members of *The Lotus Society,* who have contributed to the Endowment Fund either as an outright or estate-planned gift.

Despite Lotusland's appearance, it is not affluent. Every year is a struggle to raise the funds necessary to preserve and share Ganna Walska's vision. Maintaining a 37-acre garden and property is a massive commitment and the over 100 year old buildings and grounds require a considerable investment. The path to financial sustainability is through growing the endowment to support the care and tending of the Garden well into the future.

LOTUSLAND'S SPECTACULAR GARDENS and dramatic landscapes create an inspirational botanical wonderland, but Lotusland is much more than just a pretty place. The Garden is uniquely positioned to increase awareness and appreciation of plants and to connect people with nature. Lotusland also functions as a life raft for threatened species, acting as an insurance policy against extinction. These globally important plant collections are very diverse. There are 3,400 types of plants and approximately 35,000 individuals that are often massed in large quantities. There are many globally important plant collections at Lotusland but the most relevant in terms of science, research, conservation and education are the cycads. The cycad collection is part of the American Public Garden Association's Plant Collections Network's multi-site cycad collection. Lotusland collaborates with colleagues in South Africa on species survival plans for *Encephalartos heenanii*, a cycad that is now believed to be extinct in the wild, and to establish an assurance colony at Lotusland.

Although Lotusland is a place of much needed respite in this increasingly noisy world, there is much work that goes on that is not apparent to the public. The role of Lotusland's plant collections, though beautiful, are increasingly important on a global scale.

Since the 1990s, the Lotusland team has committed itself to the art of sustainable horticulture and, as a result, manages a larger, healthier, and more resilient garden than ever. Sustainable horticulture is simply, growing plants the way Mother Nature intended. The soil is respected, never compacted, and only organic fertilizers, composts, and mulches are applied. Building on these principles, the garden has developed a protective armor of biology where soil organisms, insects, spiders, and other animals thrive and balance the ecology of the soil while naturally managing pests.

Sustainable horticulture taps into nature's feedback loops — healthy soil begets healthy plants, begets healthy insects, begets healthy bird life — to optimize plant growth and health. More specifically, this is done by nourishing the soil and the microbes that thrive there via extensive composting and mulching, and by encouraging beneficial insects via insectary plantings that provide year-round pollen and nectar for pollinating insects and birds. Such an environment naturally manages disease and small pests.

Sustainable horticulture matters for Lotusland and the world, because it's a non-toxic method for ornamental landscape management and food production. Sustainable horticulture, and Lotusland's practice of this art, proves that partnering with nature is good for the Garden *and* the planet

Today, Lotusland manages its 37 acres using a smaller team and less water than it did in 1990s. Nature does a lot of the work. The garden benefits from the expanded insectary plantings throughout the property, the additions of mulches and compost, and brewing and spraying of thousands of gallons of compost tea.

One need not manage dozens of acres to garden sustainably. Even the smallest plots benefit from healthy soil. Lotusland encourages gardeners and farmers to heighten their sensitivity to nature, to learn to read the book Mother Nature has put in front of us.

THERE'S NO PLACE ON EARTH like Ganna Walska Lotusland–a community jewel, a botanical nirvana, a beloved public treasure.

Lotusland wishes to thank and acknowledge our Lotusland Family–our Members, donors, volunteers, staff, and visitors. Your generosity sustains the grounds and gardens, and our programs and projects. Thank you for making possible transformative educational opportunities and year round garden conservation and stewardship. Gifts enable our horticultural team to maintain the property, as well as its incredible collections of plants and trees, along with its unparalleled garden design and aesthetics. Your thoughtfulness inspires connection between nature, inspiration, and creative innovation. With your support and visitation, the Garden will remain a source of respite and well-being. Please know how sincerely grateful we are for all that you help us accomplish.

Lotusland is more than a beautiful place – it is a porthole to history, an important link in global plant preservation, a center for learning and a refuge for unparalleled spiritual elevation.

For more information, please visit our website, call us, or write to:

GANNA WALSKA LOTUSLAND
695 Ashley Road
Santa Barbara, California 93108
Office Phone 805.969.3767
Reservations 805.969.9990
www.lotusland.org

Ganna Walska Lotusland is a 501(c)(3) non-profit public charity, tax ID #23-7082550. Donations are tax-deductible as allowable by law.